The
Fearless
Four

Other titles in the Hodder African Readers series

The Fearless Four	978 0340 940426
The Fearless Four: Hijack!	978 0340 940419
The Fearless Four and the Graveyard Ghost	978 0340 940358
The Fearless Four and the Smugglers	978 0340 940334
Dead Men's Bones	978 0340 940365
Twin Trouble	978 0340 940310
Sauna and the Drug Pedlars	978 0340 940402
The Power of Corruption	978 0340 940341
Magic, Mystery and Mister Prince	978 0340 940389
Time Bomb	978 0340 940327
God's Case: No Appeal	978 0340 940372
One Man, Two Votes	978 0340 940396

The Fearless Four

John Hare

AN HACHETTE UK COMPANY

Orders: please contact Hachette UK Distribution, Hely Hutchinson Centre,
Milton Road, Didcot, Oxfordshire, OX11 7HH. Telephone: +44 (0)1235 827827.
Email: education@hachette.co.uk. Lines are open from 9 a.m. to 5 p.m., Monday to Friday.
You can also order through our website: www.hoddereducation.com

Hachette UK's policy is to use papers that are natural, renewable and recyclable products and made from wood grown in well-managed forests and other controlled sources. The logging and manufacturing processes are expected to conform to the environmental regulations of the country of origin.

All rights reserved. Apart from any use permitted under UK copyright law, no part of this publication may be reproduced or transmitted in any form or by any means, electronic or mechanical, including photocopying and recording, or held within any information storage and retrieval system, without permission in writing from the publisher or under licence from the Copyright Licensing Agency Limited. Further details of such licences (for reprographic reproduction) may be obtained from the Copyright Licensing Agency Limited, www.cla.co.uk

The authorised representative in the EEA is Hachette Ireland, 8 Castlecourt Centre, Dublin 15, D15 XTP3, Ireland (email: info@hbgi.ie)

© John Hare 1996, 2006
First published in this edition in 2006 by Hodder Education,
An Hachette UK Company
Carmelite House
50 Victoria Embankment
London EC4Y 0DZ

www.hoddereducation.com

Impression number 10 9 8 7 6

Year 2025

Cover illustration by Roger Payne

Typeset in 12/14 Bembo by Datapage India Pvt Ltd

Printed and bound in Great Britain by Clays Ltd, Elcograf S.p.A.

A catalogue record for this title is available from the British Library

ISBN: 978 0 340 94042 6

Contents

1	Tiny in Trouble	1
2	An Evil Plan	13
3	What Went Wrong?	27
4	Susan on the Trail	37
5	A Dangerous Place	48
6	What a Hero!	61
7	Well Done, Fearless Four	71

1
Tiny in Trouble

'If it hadn't been for that stupid Mr Juroge, we'd have won the match.'

'What do you mean?' Ken Kubwa looked up at his tall friend, Tiny Tantille. They were walking back to the changing room after their school team, Westview Academy, had drawn one-one in the semi-final of the township schools' cup.

'Didn't you see him?' asked Tiny, staring down at Ken. 'He got in the way of my match-winning shot. I ran down the wing, side-stepped their full back, drew their keeper out of his goal – and then what happens? Mr Juroge runs straight in front of me and blocks my shot. We miss a certain goal and draw the match. You must have seen it.'

'But I'm the goalie – I can't see everything from where I stand,' replied Ken. 'When the ball is up at the far end of the field, I take a break.'

'Well I think that Mr Juroge should be banned from refereeing our matches,' said Tiny Tantille with feeling. 'He doesn't know what he's doing.'

At that moment a hand was laid on Tiny's shoulder. He turned round and looked up into the furious face of Mr Juroge himself.

'Would you like to repeat what you have just said about me?' the teacher demanded.

'Oh, sir. I'm sorry, sir,' stammered Tiny. 'I didn't mean it, sir. I'm sure that it was an accident, sir.'

'I will see you in the staff room at five o'clock,' said Mr Juroge, trying hard to control his temper. 'I have never heard such insolence in all my life. Don't be late.'

'No, sir.'

Mr Juroge strode off across the soccer pitch and back towards the school buildings.

'Now I'm for it,' said Tiny.

'He can't do anything to you if what you said was true. He blocked your scoring shot, didn't he?'

'But he won't see it that way. He heard me being rude about him.'

'Well, in spite of the draw we're through to the cup final on goal average,' said Ken, trying hard to encourage his friend. 'As long as he doesn't stop you from playing in the final in three weeks' time, it doesn't really matter what he does to you.'

But unfortunately, that's exactly what Mr Juroge did do. He knew that nothing would hurt Tiny more than a ban on playing in the vital match.

'But, sir . . .' Tiny stammered when he was told what his punishment was to be. 'I'd rather you did anything to me than stop me from playing in the final.'

'I know, and that's why I am banning you,' said Mr Juroge with a smile.

'But what about the school, sir? Don't you want Westview to win the cup?'

Mr Juroge hesitated for a moment. 'Of course I want us to win the cup. We all want to see the school win. But your rudeness is unforgivable. Discipline at this school is more important than winning soccer matches. It's the only way I can teach you a lesson that you'll never forget.'

And that was that. Mr Juroge opened the door and told Tiny Tantille to leave the room. He was not prepared to discuss the matter any more.

Later that evening after supper Tiny went round to Ken Kubwa's house to tell him the terrible news.

'Hey, what's the matter with you, man?' asked Mrs Kubwa when she saw Tiny's sad face. She was short and plump like her son Ken and nearly always had a big smile on her face. Now the smile had disappeared and she was looking serious. 'You look as though someone has done something really terrible to you.'

'Someone has, Mrs Kubwa,' said Tiny. 'He's done the worst thing in the world to me.'

'The worst thing in the world!' exclaimed Mrs Kubwa as she reached up to put an arm around Tiny. 'Whatever can that be?'

'Mr Juroge has banned me from playing in the school soccer final.'

She stared at Tiny in amazement. 'But that's terrible. You're a star player. What did you do to him?'

'I never did like that Juroge,' Mrs Kubwa said after Tiny had explained what had happened. 'He's no good at teaching English either. Ken's writing is getting worse and he's the teacher who must take the blame. Anyway, there's nothing we can do about it now. Ken's in his room with your friend Taka Taka Tom. I expect they'll make you feel better.'

'Thanks, Mrs Kubwa.'

Tiny left her and went into Ken's bedroom. His two friends were sitting on the bed.

'Juroge's banned me from playing in the final,' Tiny explained to them.

'How could he? Doesn't he care about the school?' asked Taka Taka Tom.

'I asked him the same question. He just said that discipline in the school was more important than winning soccer matches,' Tiny replied.

Taka Taka Tom was not in the Westview soccer team. He was not particularly good at

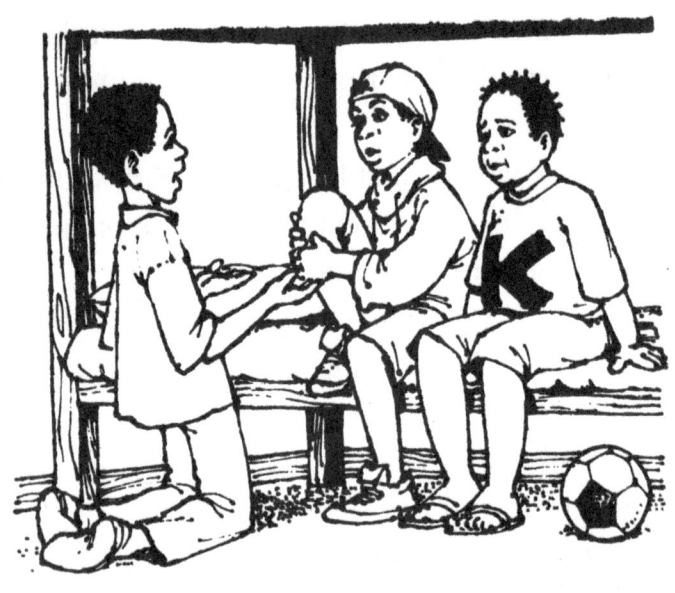

anything but he was a loyal friend of the two boys.

'Let's go down to the Daystar,' said Ken. 'My little brothers will be back soon and it's easier to talk down there. At least it's Saturday tomorrow. You don't have to go to school and see that idiot Juroge.'

The Daystar was a popular eating house about half a kilometre away. The boys often met there to escape from their overcrowded houses. They left Ken's house and walked along the narrow street towards the Daystar. It had rained the night before and water had collected in the many pot-holes in the road. Tiny didn't try to avoid getting his feet wet. He splashed through the pot-holes, his hands in his pockets, his shoulders hunched.

'Hey, Tiny, did you win your match?' a friend of his father's called out from the verandah of an old wooden house. Rusty pieces of tin roofing sheets flapped up and down in the wind. 'Did you win, man?' he shouted again above the noise of the banging roofing sheets.

'No, we drew,' Tiny called.

'Well that's better than losing,' the man shouted back.

'But it's not as good as winning,' Tiny muttered to himself.

'Come on, Tiny,' said Ken, trying to encourage him. 'It's not as bad as all that.'

'Oh, yes it is,' replied Tiny.

They had reached the Daystar and Taka Taka Tom pushed his way through the strings of plastic beads that covered the entrance. They walked into a courtyard, open to the sky. The eating house was empty except for three men who were arguing loudly by the bar. The boys sat down at a metal table, ordered three Cokes and began to talk among themselves about what had happened to Tiny. Soon, though, the argument became so noisy they had to stop.

'I know the All Stars will win,' said a fat man wearing a brightly-coloured shirt and a hat perched on the back of his head. 'I know it, I know it,' he repeated, banging his fist down on the wooden counter of the bar. This made a beer bottle fall down and smash to pieces on the concrete floor.

'Know it, Joe? How can you possibly know it?' asked his equally fat companion, ignoring the crash and the broken glass at his feet. The third man was tall, thin and hawk-like and wore a smart suit. He stared at the broken bottle but said nothing.

At this point the owner of the Daystar, a large woman with a fat pudgy face, came out from behind a torn curtain. She wiped her hands vigorously on a dirty red and white apron that was tied around her waist.

'Hey, stop this brawling,' she cried out. 'Stop it at once or I'll turn you all out of here. I don't want any fighting in the Daystar. We've a good reputation round here and no strangers are going to spoil it.'

'We're not going to start a fight,' said Joe, pushing back his hat even further. 'I'm just saying that I know something this jelly-belly here doesn't know.'

'Jelly-belly? Jelly-belly? Now you're getting personal.' The other big man picked up a piece of broken glass and held it in front of Joe's face.

The thin man, who until now had been silent, grabbed the man's hand and forced it away from Joe.

'Don't be stupid,' he hissed. 'If you start fighting in here she'll call the police.'

'I sure will,' said Annie, the owner of the Daystar. 'They're parked just round the corner. You'll be bundled into their van before you can say All Star soccer club. If you so much as touch each other I'll be straight on to my portable phone.'

She gave a toss of her head, wagged her finger in their faces, and disappeared behind the ragged curtain.

'That was close,' muttered Tiny as the men got up to leave. 'I thought things were going to get nasty.'

As the three men walked past their table, Taka Taka took a good look at them. "They look like strangers to me,' he said to the others. 'I've never seen them in the Daystar before. They've most likely come here for the big match.'

'I don't know why that fat man was so confident the All Stars will win tomorrow,' said Ken. 'The Black Eagles are very good. Everyone thinks that they're the better team. Their goalkeeper Shomate is my hero. He's amazing and the best player they've got. I'd like to be able to play like him one day. I'm sure that the Black Eagles will win.'

'It's going to be a great match,' said Taka Taka Tom. 'My dad says that two teams from the same township haven't met in a final for over thirty years.'

'We should go there early or we won't get in,' said Tiny. For the first time he had forgotten his own troubles. 'Shall we meet here at two o'clock tomorrow? That will give us an hour and a half before the kick-off.'

'Susan wants to come with us,' said Taka Taka, looking at each of his friends in turn. 'Should we let her come?'

Tiny and Ken stared at each other.

'What? Are you asking us to go to the match with a *girl?*' asked Ken. 'You can't be serious.'

Susan Saito went to Westview Academy with the boys. They all liked her and sometimes she was useful to them. But it was quite another thing for her to go with them to a soccer match.

'It's not possible,' said Tiny. 'We can't go with a girl.'

Taka Taka looked disappointed.

'Are you going soft or something?' asked Ken. 'Soft in the head, I mean?'

'OK,' said Taka Taka with a sigh. 'I'll tell her what you said.'

Ken stared at him. 'I think you really are going soft,' he exclaimed.

The boys finished their Cokes and left the Daystar. At least Tiny Tantille had something to take his mind off being dropped from the school soccer team. The final of the township league between the All Stars and the Black Eagles.

2
An Evil Plan

The three boys met at the Daystar at two o'clock the next day. Annie gave them all a free Coke before they left and they set off in good spirits. The soccer ground was on the outskirts of the town and they had to wait for a bus to take them there. When the bus eventually arrived it was so over-crowded that they thought there wouldn't be enough room for them to get on board. People pushed their way on until the bus was carrying twice as many passengers as it should have done.

The battered old vehicle had run up and down the township roads for fifteen years. It creaked and groaned as it bumped over the potholes on its way to the soccer stadium. Every time the bus stopped more people shoved on board. No one got off. Everyone was going to the soccer match. The three boys had been pushed into the middle of the bus. They couldn't move and they could hardly breathe.

At long last the bus reached the stadium and the passengers surged towards the two exit doors. The boys were swept along with everybody else and moments later they were squeezed out of the bus.

'That was some ride,' said Tiny, who had been able to see over the heads of the other passengers.

'It's all right for you,' panted Ken. The sweat was running down his face and he was gasping for breath. 'You carry your head in the clouds but I get my face stuffed into everybody's belly.'

Taka Taka laughed. 'Let's go,' he said. 'Let's get into the stadium as fast as we can. They might shut the gates soon.'

The boys ran towards a queue of people who were lining up to pay their money. Each person had to pass through an iron gate, one at a time. They queued for fifteen minutes and at last reached the gate. Ken, who had collected all their money, put his hand in his pocket. His pocket was empty! His purse had been stolen.

'My pocket's been picked,' he cried out. 'The money has gone.' He looked around at his friends in dismay.

'Are you sure?' asked Tiny.

'Of course I am. It's gone.'

'Are you two boys going to pay or not?' the man at the gate asked rudely. 'If you've got no money then leave the queue.'

'Yes, leave the queue,' shouted someone behind them.

'Don't waste our time,' said another man impatiently.

'Those boys are trying to get in free,' someone else shouted out.

'Get out! Run along. We want to go in.'

Ken looked helplessly at his two friends.

'You had all our money,' said Taka Taka. 'We've got nothing. You know that.'

Someone grabbed Ken by the arm and pulled him away from the front of the queue. The people behind surged forward and the three boys were forced out of the line.

'What can we do?' asked Ken. 'My purse must have been stolen in the bus.'

The boys walked sadly away from the queue. It was now a lot longer than when they had first joined it.

'Unless we find someone who knows us, we'll never get in,' said Ken.

'Everything is going wrong at the moment,' muttered Tiny gloomily.

Heads down, they made their way around the outside of the stadium. Queues of people stretched in all directions. If they didn't join a queue soon they would never get in. The gates would be closed.

'Look, there's Susan!' shouted Taka Taka suddenly.

'Where?'

'Over there. Near the front of that queue.'

The boys looked in the direction he was pointing. They saw Susan, with her young brother, standing near the front of one of the queues.

'Maybe she has some money that she can lend us,' said Taka Taka.

He ran up to her and explained what had happened.

'I don't see why I should lend you any money at all,' Susan said, rather crossly. 'After all, you refused to let me come with you. Why should I help you now?'

'Please, Susan. Please.'

'Oh, all right,' she said. 'It's lucky for you I've brought all the pocket money I've saved up. And I suppose you want to join me in the queue as well.'

Ken and Tiny had already edged into the queue behind Susan but the people behind her soon started to complain.

'What do you boys think you're doing?'

'Go to the back of the line. We've been here for half an hour.'

'Get out of it.'

A man pushed Tiny roughly out of the way.

Luckily they had just reached the entrance gate. Susan handed the clerk enough money for all five of them to get in. Click-click-click-click-click. They all passed through.

Ignoring the angry shouts behind them, the three boys ran with Susan and her young brother Timo towards the stands.

'Thanks, Susan,' said Ken. 'That was really good of you.'

'It's more than can be said of you! Why didn't you let me come with you?' replied Susan. 'I thought we were friends.'

'We are friends, but you're a girl,' said Tiny. 'There's some places you can go with a girl and there are others that you cannot. You know that.'

'I don't know it. I don't accept it and I never will,' Susan replied hotly. 'One day I'll prove you all wrong.'

They entered the stands and managed to find seats on one of the old wooden benches. They had quite a good view of the stadium. There were twenty minutes to go before the match was due to begin.

'I think I'll just go to the toilet,' said Taka Taka Tom. 'I'm bursting.'

'OK, but don't get lost.'

'Don't worry, I won't.'

'We're in C2, Row 33,' Ken shouted out as Taka Taka pushed his way back towards the entrance to the stands.

'I don't know whether he heard that,' said Tiny.

'Well, too bad if he didn't,' said Ken crossly. 'He should have gone to the toilet before he came in here.'

Taka Taka Tom forced his way through the crowd of people still coming in. There was nothing he could do. He had to go to the toilet. The toilet block was some way away from the entrance to stand C2 and it took him a while to find it. He relieved himself and started to walk back. Unfortunately he hadn't heard the number that Ken had called out to him and before long he was lost. The ground was completely full. Although the gates were now closed, people were clambering over the top of the high walls all around the ground. It didn't seem to matter that the walls were topped with broken glass. The police just stood and watched them climb over.

'Now where are we?' muttered Taka Taka to himself. 'I think it's this one.' He turned towards a stadium entrance and climbed some stairs. It looked different from before. He couldn't understand why there were so few people about.

In fact, Taka Taka Tom had entered the players' entrance without anybody noticing him.

In a very short time he was utterly confused. He didn't know where he was. What he did know was that he had taken the wrong entrance.

Just as he turned to go back he spotted someone whom he recognised. It was the fat man who had been boasting in the Daystar that the All Stars would win. What is he doing here? Taka Taka wondered. The man looked agitated and was hurrying down a corridor that led under the stadium. Taka Taka made up his mind to follow him.

He often wondered why he decided to do this. Why hadn't he retraced his steps, and tried to find the correct entrance to his stand? Later he would say that he felt the fat man called Joe was up to no good. But really it was just curiosity. He had seen the man before, he had heard him boasting in the Daystar. Now he wanted to find out just what he was up to.

Joe walked towards a door with a large red cross painted on the outside. It must be the medical room, thought Taka Taka. The place where they treat injured players.

Joe entered the room. The door banged behind him but did not close. Taka Taka crouched down and peered through the half-open door.

'Did you do it, Doc?' asked Joe. 'Did you fix him?'

'I'll say I did,' a man answered. 'He thought he was getting a pain-killer. Just wait until he gets out on the pitch. He won't know what's hit him.'

'Good,' said Joe. 'Well done. That's fixed it, then.'

'You should get out of here,' said the man he'd called Doc. 'The match starts soon and there will be questions asked if they find you in here.'

'OK, Doc,' said Joe.

'What about my fee?'

'All in good time,' replied Joe with a laugh. 'You'll get it all right. When the Black Eagles have lost the match.'

Taka Taka gasped as he realised what he had just heard. The doctor was in the pay of Joe. He had given some kind of injection to a key player who thought it was a pain-killer.

Suddenly he heard a footstep behind him and as he turned to run away he was roughly grabbed by both arms. It was the thin man who had been in the Daystar. The man who was called Croesus, and had stopped Joe from being hit with the broken bottle.

'What do you think you're doing here?' asked Croesus, twisting one of Taka Taka's arms until he cried out with pain.

'Who's there?' Joe called out. 'Who is it?'

'It's me, Joe,' the thin man called out. 'It's Croesus.'

Joe had walked to the door. 'Who have you caught, Cro?' he asked.

'This boy's been spying on you,' Croesus said.

Joe hit Taka Taka on the head with the flat of his hand.

'Let me go,' Taka Taka yelled.

'This kid will ruin us all. Quick – bring him inside before someone hears him.'

The two men bundled Taka Taka Tom into the medical room.

'Give him a fix with the same drug, Doc,' Joe ordered. 'And be quick about it.'

Taka Taka bit Croesus on the hand. Joe gave him another slap with his right hand as the doctor came up to him with a syringe and a needle.

'Stop it! Stop it!' yelled Taka Taka. This time Joe didn't hit him as he struggled. He wrapped his great palm around his mouth.

'Hold his arm out,' the doctor ordered.

They forced Taka Taka's arm out in front of the doctor, who plunged the needle into it. 'That will fix him. He will be asleep in seconds.'

Moments later, Taka Taka Tom went limp and slumped in the arms of Croesus. From the roar that could be heard from outside the room, it was obvious that the soccer match had started.

'That dose was three times the amount that I gave Shomate,' said the doctor. 'Shomate will only seem fuddled. This boy will be out for three hours at least.'

'What shall we do with him?' Joe asked.

'We can't leave him here. You may be getting an injured player through the door at any moment,' Croesus said to the doctor.

Joe thought for a while. 'Carry him out of the ground, Croesus,' he said. 'Pretend he's your son and that he's fainted with all the excitement. Kids do that all the time. No one will ask you any questions.'

Croesus picked up Taka Taka and slung him over his shoulder.

'You can say that you brought him to the Doc here for treatment. He's certainly been given some,' Joe said with a cruel laugh.

'Who is he?' the doctor asked.

'I've no idea. Some township kid, I think. No one will miss him.'

'Are you going to dump him?' asked the doctor.

'That's much too dangerous,' Croesus replied. 'He's seen and heard too much. We've got to take him to a safe house and then we can worry about what to do with him.'

There was another great roar from outside.

'I want to see this match,' said Joe. 'No point in staying here. It sounds as though there's great excitement out there and I can guess who is causing it,' he added with a chuckle.

'I'll take our young friend away,' Croesus said grimly. 'Joe, follow me by taxi when the match is over. You know where I'll be.'

3
What Went Wrong?

Meanwhile, Susan, Ken and Tiny were more concerned with what was happening in the match than worrying about Taka Taka Tom.

The All Stars were winning by two goals to nil after only ten minutes' play. The Black Eagles were playing much better than the All Stars but Shomate had missed two easy saves. Ken in particular was very upset to see his hero play so badly.

'I could have saved those goals,' he said to Tiny. 'What's the matter with Shomate?'

The doctor had given Shomate just enough of the drug to affect him, but not enough for him to know what was wrong. He appeared to be watching the play and following what was going on. However, when the ball came towards him, his vision blurred and he couldn't see it properly. The crowd could not detect that he had been drugged. All they could see was the terrible way that he was playing.

Some of the Black Eagle supporters were already beginning to shout at their former hero. Shomate was jogging on the spot in an effort to pull himself together.

All at once the Black Eagles took possession of the ball and ran with it up the right wing. The winger passed to the centre-forward who tapped it back to the centre-half. The centre-half made a perfect pass to the left-winger, who immediately swung it back towards the centre-forward. This was more like it. The supporters of the Black Eagles roared happily at this dazzling play.

The centre-forward ran up, side-stepped the All Star left-back and shot hard at goal. The supporters' roar of approval at his brilliant move turned to groans as the ball hit the cross-bar of the All Star goal.

'Bad luck,' shouted Tiny excitedly. 'That was real bad luck.'

The ball bounced back into play and the All Star centre-half scooped it up and kicked it down the length of the pitch. This was a stroke of desperation as none of the All Star forwards were in the Black Eagles' half. The ball rolled gently up to the Eagle right-back.

When that happens, the player often just taps it back to the goalkeeper. The keeper then runs forward and boots it down the field to one of his team mates.

The right-back half turned and tapped the ball back towards Shomate. 'Give it a good boot up the field,' he shouted. 'We've got them on the run. Kick it as hard as you can.'

The ball trickled slowly towards Shomate, who moved towards the ball to kick it. But first to the amazement and then to the horror of the crowd, he failed to do so. The ball trickled through Shomate's legs and into the Black Eagle goal.

The All Star fans went wild.

'Own goal! Own goal!' they hooted.

Against all the run of the play the All Stars were winning three-nil.

'There's something wrong with Shomate,' Susan said. She looked up anxiously at Ken

and Tiny. 'I'm sure there's something the matter with him. Even I could have stopped that.'

'Anyone could have stopped it,' said Ken heatedly.

'It's crazy,' shouted Tiny. 'What's the matter with him?' Then he suddenly remembered Taka Taka Tom. 'What do you think has happened to Taka Taka?' he asked. 'He should have been back here a long time ago.'

'I expect he's got lost. He'll be watching the match from some other stand,' said Ken.

'That's not like him,' said Susan. 'He never gives up. I am sure that he would have gone on searching until he found us.'

But soon they all stopped worrying about Taka Taka Tom. For the moment, what was happening on the playing field was much more important.

The Black Eagle captain had come up to Shomate and was talking earnestly to him. Shomate was shaking his head as though insisting that he was all right. The captain then went up to the referee. He was asking if he could change Shomate's position in the team.

'Not until half-time,' the referee replied. 'That's the rule. No changes can be made until half-time.'

By half-time the score was four-one to the All Stars. Shomate had let in another goal from what would normally have been a simple save. The Black Eagles had scored once but the whole side was dragged down by the performance of Shomate. They were playing well below their best. When the half-time whistle was blown the Black Eagle supporters yelled and jeered at poor Shomate, who returned to the dressing room hanging his head in shame.

In the second half the Black Eagle captain brought on another goalkeeper. Poor Shomate was asked to play left-half. But the angry Black Eagle supporters would rather he hadn't come back on to the field at all. They would have preferred their team to play with only ten men, rather than have Shomate making error after error.

But Shomate had insisted on playing. 'There's nothing wrong with me,' he told his captain. 'You watch me this half. I'll win the match for you.'

Against his better judgement, the captain allowed him to play.

The second half started badly for the All Stars. The determined Black Eagles attacked and attacked and eventually they were rewarded with two goals one after the other. Their supporters urged them on. If they could keep up this attacking pace then they could still beat the All Stars, in spite of the disasters of the first half.

'Come on, Eagles!' yelled Ken and Tiny. 'Come on, come on.'

They had all forgotten about Taka Taka. The excitement of the match had made certain of that.

When the All Stars did manage a shot at goal the reserve goalkeeper stopped it with ease. Poor Shomate was a passenger. He ran up and down the pitch in a daze. Sometimes he tried a half-hearted tackle but the All Star player always managed to beat him to the ball. The Eagles could still win, even with Shomate on the field – as long as he didn't do anything stupid.

A great run by the Black Eagle centre-half burst through the All Star defence. He kicked a long curving shot and the ball fizzed past the All Star goalkeeper and found the back of the net. The crowd went wild. There was just half a minute before the final whistle, and the score was level at four-four. The game would have to go into the ten minutes of extra time. The referee blew three long blasts on his whistle and the second half was over.

The sides changed ends and the match went on. The game continued at the same furious pace, with the Black Eagles making one attack after another. One shot hit the cross-bar. Another hit the upright. People were urging their teams to victory with a mighty roar that could be heard all over the township.

Suddenly the ball was passed to Shomate. 'Now,' the unfortunate player said to himself. 'Now you can do it.' He summoned all his strength and ran as fast as he could, dribbling the ball towards the goal. There seemed to be a huge empty space in front of him and the crowd was roaring in his ears. But they weren't urging him on. They were shouting at him. Yelling at him. Screaming at him. 'Wrong goal, Shomate! The other goal, Shomate!'

Poor Shomate. In his drugged state he hadn't remembered that for the vital ten minutes of extra time the two teams had changed ends. He was running with the ball towards his own goal.

The Black Eagle reserve goalkeeper was yelling at him as he approached. 'Don't shoot, you fool. Give me the ball. Kick it to me.'

But Shomate was completely confused. The roar from the crowd and the words from his own goalkeeper meant nothing to him. He was going to show everyone that the mistakes he had made in the first half could be put right. He would score the winning goal for his team. He would. He would.

Suddenly the crowd fell strangely silent as the 80,000 spectators realised what was about to happen. They couldn't believe their eyes. Shomate suddenly stopped, drew back his right foot and booted the ball as hard as he could, straight towards his own goal.

The reserve goalkeeper dived to his right to deflect the shot. Maybe Shomate on a good day would have saved it. But for a reserve it was impossible. The ball bounced off his outstretched hands and into the net. Shomate leapt in the air and turned to receive the congratulations of his colleagues. He heard a whistle being blown. The match was over.

'We've won,' he shouted out. 'We've won and I've done it. I've scored the winning goal.' If his colleagues wouldn't congratulate him he would congratulate himself. He hugged himself in utter delight. He couldn't understand why he wasn't being carried shoulder-high to the dressing-room.

What was the matter with everybody? What was wrong? Why were the crowd yelling at him? Why were some spectators running angrily towards him? What had happened?

A furious young Black Eagle supporter suddenly drew level with him. 'You swine,' he called out. 'You pig. You …'

The spectator clenched his fist, swung his right arm and hit Shomate hard on the chin. As Shomate sank to the ground, dazed and confused, the spectator kicked him.

Moments later police arrived on the scene. They surrounded Shomate to prevent other angry supporters from attacking him. After arresting the spectator, they escorted the injured Shomate all the way to the dressing-room. Not one of his team-mates spoke to him. Each player looked at Shomate with hatred in his eyes. They had given their all, only to have one of their own players snatch victory from their grasp.

4
Susan on the Trail

After the excitement of the match, the boys and Susan once again remembered Taka Taka.

'He'll find his own way home,' said Ken.

'Don't forget he hasn't got any money,' said Susan. 'It's a long way to his house and I wouldn't like to get near those Eagle supporters. They are so angry that they might well riot.'

'Or try to kill Shomate.'

'What was the matter with him?' Tiny wondered.

'I think something had happened to him,' said Susan thoughtfully. 'He looked as though he might have been drugged.'

Ken suddenly remembered the stranger in the Daystar who had been boasting that he knew the All Stars would win. He told Susan all about him.

'A lot of people bet money on soccer matches,' Susan said. 'If a side that is expected to lose suddenly wins, then some people make a pile of money.'

'Do you think the man they called Joe knew that the match was going to be fixed?'

'I don't know, but I'll tell you something that I've just remembered,' exclaimed Tiny excitedly.

'What's that?' asked Ken.

'I read in the *Comet* that Shomate was injured in a league game last week. An opposing player kicked him on the knee. It was touch and go whether he would play today. They said he was on pain-killers.'

'Hmm,' said Susan thoughtfully. 'Someone could have been paid to injure him.'

'Well, it didn't work – he played in the end.'

'But look *how* he played. Do you think it was normal, the way he behaved? He didn't know where he was or what he was doing.'

They had reached the exit gate. Some of the Black Eagle supporters were chanting slogans and they weren't pleasant ones. It seemed as though they were ready to kill Shomate if they could get hold of him.

'I think we had better get home as soon as possible,' Ken began and then stopped suddenly. 'Look over there. That's him. That's the man who was in the Daystar. What do you think he's up to?'

The man was getting into a black Toyota. It pulled away from a line of other battered taxis.

Susan reacted in a flash. 'Take little Timo,' she said. 'I'm going to follow them.'

'You're crazy,' said Ken. 'They could be dangerous.'

'I have the money, don't I?' said Susan with a laugh. She stuffed a bank note into Ken's hand to give him enough money to get them all home.

'I'll be all right,' she said as she ran towards the taxi rank. 'I'm only a girl, you know. You said yourself that there were certain places you wouldn't go with a girl.'

Ken started to run after her but Tiny held him back. 'Let her go,' he said. 'It's too late to stop her, anyway.'

Indeed it was. Susan had already climbed into a taxi that was pulling away from the curb. The large crowd that was streaming away from the stadium stopped the cars from travelling fast. Ken saw some people banging on the top of the taxis to work off their anger about the match. It was going to be a wild night in the township. Timo started to cry.

'Don't worry, Timo,' said Tiny, picking the little boy up and setting him on his shoulders. 'We'll get you home safely long before Susan comes back.'

'I'm not worried about that! I'm worried about my sister,' said Timo. 'What is she doing? Where is she going?'

Both Ken and Tiny were worried about Susan. They also had to look after Timo and there was only one thing they could do. Get him home as fast as possible.

'Susan's given us enough money for a taxi but I think we should go by bus, even though we'll all be squashed. I don't want to travel in a taxi through the township tonight. It's safer on the bus,' said Tiny.

They walked over to a line of people who were waiting to leave. Luckily, two buses drew up one after the other and without too much difficulty they clambered aboard the second one. Ken clutched Susan's money tightly in his clenched fist. He wasn't going to take any chances.

Meanwhile, Susan's driver was doing his best to follow the black Toyota that carried Joe.

Angry faces peered in at her through the windows of the taxi.

'You lock the doors, missie,' said the driver. 'You don't know what those guys will do.'

Susan's heart was pounding but she bravely told the driver to keep going.

'The crowd must thin out soon,' she said. 'Then you'll be able to drive normally.'

'There's going to be no normal driving in this town tonight, missie,' replied the taxi driver. 'There's only going to be trouble. Big trouble. I can smell it coming like the first rains after a drought. Why, these people are not just angry. They're furious! If they catch

Shomate they will pull him apart limb by limb. What I tell you is true.'

'I know, I know,' said Susan desperately as another fist banged down on the top of the cab. 'But maybe it wasn't his fault.'

'Not his fault? What do you mean?' The taxi driver turned round and stared at her in disbelief. 'Of course it was his fault.'

The crowd had nearly gone. They were able to travel faster.

'Don't lose that car in front, whatever you do. Don't let him see that we're following him,' ordered Susan.

The Toyota gathered speed. They were driving away from the township and out into the open countryside.

'He could be going on for another hundred kilometres,' said the driver moodily. 'I hope you've got enough money in your purse, missie.'

'I told you I'd pay you your money, however far you take me. I brought all my money with me. We were going to celebrate after the match.'

The taxi driver looked round at her in surprise. Has she really got that much money? he thought to himself.

Susan looked back over her shoulder. The sky behind them glowed red and she saw flames leaping into the sky. 'Look,' she cried out. 'They are setting houses in the township on fire.'

'I've already told you, missie, there's going to be plenty of trouble in the township tonight. It hasn't even started yet. Not by a long way.'

'I hope Timo will be all right,' Susan said softly. She suddenly felt guilty at having left her young brother.

'What's that?'

'Nothing. I was just talking to myself.'

'It takes all sorts,' said the driver. 'And I seem to get all sorts in my cab.'

'Can you still see the car in front? I've lost it.'

'Yes, it's still there and travelling fast. Hey, wait a minute. It seems to have turned off into the bush.'

They came to an unmade track where the Toyota had turned off.

'Am I supposed to go down that?' asked the taxi driver in disgust. 'That path is like a mountain range. It'll break up my car in five minutes.'

'Not if you drive slowly it won't,' replied Susan, as practical as ever. 'Just you take it easy and follow those Toyota tracks. I can see the tyre marks quite clearly, so even if they pull ahead of us we can follow them. But keep your lights dimmed. We don't want them to spot us.'

'Yes ma'am,' said the driver. 'You're going to be some madam when you grow up, I can see that,' he added.

Susan ignored the remark. 'Go slowly,' she said. 'They mustn't see us.'

After about five kilometres they saw the lights of a house ahead of them.

'That's where they are,' said Susan. 'You can drop me here. It's too dangerous for us to go any closer. And turn your lights off, so the other taxi doesn't see you. I want you to wait for me. I'll give you half your money now and the other half when I come back.'

'No, no, no, little missie,' said the taxi driver with a laugh. 'You give me all my money now. I'll wait for you. If you don't come back then I've still got my money, haven't I?'

Susan didn't know what to do. If she gave the man all the money now he might drive away. She might never see him again. However, she could see quite clearly that he wasn't going to accept half his money.

'Please, don't let me down,' she said as she handed over her precious savings. 'Please wait for me. I have to trust somebody.'

The driver was not a bad man. He thought his young passenger was crazy but he admired her courage.

'Don't you worry,' he said. 'I'll wait for you.'

'And if I don't come back in one hour, fetch the police,' she said. 'Please, do that. Will you?'

'The police! Now, that's something quite different. It's not that I'm in trouble. It's just that I don't particularly like getting involved with policemen.'

'Please, please, please,' Susan pleaded. 'Please, do as I ask.'

The taxi driver sighed. 'OK, I agree,' he said. 'I wouldn't do it for just anybody but I'll do it for you.'

'Listen,' whispered Susan. 'I could be about to discover why Shomate played so badly today. Do you understand what I'm saying?'

'Shomate? That so and so! What have you got to do with that man?'

'I think the people who live here might have drugged him or something. That's why I asked you to follow the Toyota. I may be quite wrong but somehow I don't think so.'

'What are you trying to be?' asked the taxi driver in amazement. 'A detective or something?'

'No, of course not,' said Susan impatiently. 'Look, I have to go now. Wait for me. If I'm not back in one hour call the police.' She paused a moment. 'If I am right and Shomate was drugged then you could be a hero. The match would be cancelled and there would be a replay. Then the Black Eagles will win as they should have done today.'

'You really are something else,' said the taxi driver. His eyes were open wide in amazement at what he had just been told. 'You really are. OK, I'll do just as you say.'

5
A Dangerous Place

Susan got out of the cab and walked towards the house. Luckily, there was a moon and she could see where she was going. She walked slowly along the track, carefully avoiding the overhanging branches of bushes and 'wait a bit' thorn. It seemed as though the house had been used to keep animals. There were a number of old broken-down buildings dotted about. Susan stopped by one of them. The door was half open and she could smell a strong stench of feathers and chickens. She passed another building that must have been used for keeping pigs. She was nearer the house now and she could see a car parked outside the front door.

As she passed a small brick building something flashed in the moonlight. She walked silently over to it and saw that the wooden door of the building was locked with a shiny brass padlock. It was the padlock that had winked at her.

It's new, she thought to herself. She looked at the padlock for a moment and then walked around the building. She sensed that it was used as a store. Was it her imagination or did she hear a faint noise coming from inside? Probably rats, she thought with a shudder. Susan hated rats.

There was a window set in one of the side walls but it was placed too high up for her to see inside. The moonlight was shining on to the dirty glass. Then she heard the faint noise again. I must find something to stand on, she thought.

The object that she was looking for found her! As she started her search for something to stand on, she banged her leg painfully against a piece of metal. She bit her lip in pain for the sharp metal had cut into her flesh. But she had found just what she was after. The top of an old metal wheelbarrow. She dragged it from under some tangled grass and weeds and, as quietly as she could, pulled it towards the little brick building. Moments later she had placed it under the window and had clambered on top of it.

She wiped the dirty window pane with her handkerchief and peered in. The moonlight sent a shaft of light directly through the glass. Susan thought that she could make out a bundle of old rags. Then all at once the rags moved. Not once but twice. Her heart pounded loudly in her ears. They were not rags at all. She was looking at a human body!

She jumped back down to the ground. Have I found Taka Taka Tom? she asked herself frantically. If so, how can I get him out of there?

Susan ran round to the locked door. Suddenly she remembered something that she always carried in the little bag that was stuffed into the back pocket of her jeans. Her nail-file. That might do the trick!

She took her nail-file and carefully inserted it into the lock. It twisted in the lock but it wouldn't open. Use it as a screwdriver, she thought. She inserted the blunt end into one of the six screws that held the lock in place. To her delight it started to turn. Five minutes later she had undone four of the screws. Now she was able to lever the lock from the door by inserting a piece of rusty metal between the door and the lock. The lock came away from the door frame and the door opened.

She went inside and bent down over the pile of rags. It was Taka Taka Tom.

'Taka Taka,' she whispered. 'It's me, Susan. Can you hear me?'

Taka Taka groaned. His hands were tied behind his back and his ankles were tied together. She started to undo the knots. They

had been tightly tied and it took her another ten minutes to untie them. She rubbed his wrists and ankles, murmuring all the time, 'Taka Taka. It's me, Susan.'

At last Taka Taka opened his eyes. He was still feeling the effects of the heavy dosage of the drug, but he recognized Susan. 'I'm so thirsty,' he gasped.

'I can't do anything about that now,' she whispered.

Taka Taka sat up. 'Where are we?' he asked. 'Oh, I feel so ill.'

'You must have been drugged.'

'Of course. I remember now,' said Taka Taka Tom slowly. He shook his head from side to side. He then told Susan what had happened to him after he had lost his way in the soccer stadium. 'Shomate received the same drug as me,' he added, 'but in a smaller dosage.'

'I understand everything now,' said Susan. 'Those evil men drugged Shomate so that the All Stars would win and they would make a lot of money.'

'What shall we do?' Taka Taka asked. His head was clearing and he had risen shakily to his feet.

'We must stick together,' said Susan. 'It might take some time before the effects of the drug that they gave you wear off. I asked the taxi driver who brought me here to fetch the police if I did not return in an hour. That was about thirty minutes ago.'

'Will he do it?' Taka Taka asked.

'I don't know,' Susan replied. 'We must just hope that he will. But now we need to get some proof. If we don't, the police will never believe our story. Let's go to the house. We must keep in the shadows. If Joe is in there and he finds us, he'll kill us.'

They cautiously made their way up to one side of the house. A light was shining brightly from the windows of a front room. They couldn't see inside. The curtains were tightly drawn.

'Look,' Susan whispered, pointing up at an open window. 'I can climb through that.'

The window was a small one, above a pair of larger windows that were firmly shut.

'It looks like the bathroom,' Susan said, peering through the glass. 'Can you give me a leg up, Taka Taka?'

'I'll try,' said Taka Taka. He was still feeling very shaky. Susan placed her foot in his cupped hands and he raised her up so that she was able to wriggle through the open window. She let herself silently down into the room. Then she quickly opened the larger windows beneath and Taka Taka climbed into the room beside her. Luckily, the windows had no security bars.

Susan took Taka Taka's hand and led him towards the bathroom door. She suddenly noticed something on a shelf that looked like a torch. That will be useful, she thought. She picked up the 'torch' and switched it on. It immediately began to make a noisy, whirring sound. It wasn't a torch. It was a battery shaver.

Susan hastily switched the shaver off but it was too late. She heard shouts and a door slammed. Someone was running towards the bathroom.

'Quick, get behind the door,' she said. She squeezed behind Taka Taka as the door to the bathroom was flung open. A light was switched on.

'Who's there?' a man called out. It was Croesus. He looked behind the door and stared in amazement at Susan and Taka Taka Tom.

Croesus pulled out a gun and pointed it at Taka Taka. 'Don't move,' he said, 'or you're dead. Joe – come here!'

'Well, well,' said Joe when he arrived. 'This boy can't leave us alone, can he?' He stared at Susan. 'And who are you?'

'I'm a friend of his,' said Susan defiantly, 'and I know exactly what you're up to.'

Joe's eyes narrowed. 'What do you mean?' he asked.

Without thinking what might happen to them, Susan told Joe everything she knew. 'I know what you did to Shomate. I know how you fixed the final so that the Black Eagles would lose. I know that you drugged my friend, Taka Taka Tom. I know that the soccer stadium doctor is a crook.' She stared defiantly at the two men.

'In that case,' Joe said with a snarl, 'you know much too much.' He turned towards Croesus. 'Bring them into the sitting-room, Cro. We have to do something about this. These two could ruin us.'

Croesus pushed the two children roughly out of the bathroom. His pistol was pointing at them all the time.

Joe whispered something to Croesus and Croesus laughed. 'Good idea,' he said.

'You won't get away with this,' said Susan.

'And nor will you,' said Joe coldly. 'You won't get away from here unless it's in a coffin. We'll see to that.'

Joe ordered them to sit down on two wooden chairs. Croesus handed Joe the pistol and came back moments later carrying some rope. Taka Taka hesitated for a moment and turned his head towards the open door. Immediately, Joe pointed the gun above his head and fired a shot.

The bullet thudded into the sitting-room wall and the shot echoed round the house.

'I just wanted to show you that this isn't a toy,' said Croesus. 'Just in case you were thinking of running away.'

Taka Taka Tom and Susan were now very frightened. They knew that they were in the hands of desperate men. Men who wanted to silence them for ever because they knew too much. Croesus wound the rope tightly around the two of them. He pulled the rope so tight that they cried out in pain.

'That's enough of your noise,' said Joe. 'Gag them, Cro.'

Croesus tied a piece of rag around their mouths. Neither Susan nor Taka Taka could make a sound. They were helpless.

Joe looked down at them with a cruel look in his eyes. 'I'm afraid that you two brave detectives will have to die,' he said. 'It's a pity because you are so young but I cannot risk keeping you alive. There are a number of houses burning in the township tonight. One more fire will hardly be noticed,' he added with a laugh.

'Shall I get some petrol?' asked Croesus.

'Sure, there's more than we need in your car,' replied Joe. 'Siphon some off, Cro. Not too much, though. Just enough to set this old shack alight.'

By now, Susan and Taka Taka were shaking with terror. Joe was obviously planning to burn the house down with the two of them tied up inside it. They heard the noise of the car start up as Croesus drove it a little way from the house.

For a moment Joe said nothing. Then he broke the silence. 'You will be interested to learn what we made from the bets we took on the result of the soccer match. Over a hundred thousand bucks. A cool one hundred thousand.' Joe always had to boast about his success. When the boys had met him for the first time in the Daystar they had overheard him boasting.

There was a splashing sound as Croesus threw petrol on to the walls of the house.

'Come outside, Joe,' Croesus called out. 'I don't want to roast you as well.'

'Goodbye, my darlings,' said Joe to the terrified children as he left the room. 'Sweet dreams.'

Taka Taka and Susan looked at each other and struggled briefly to free themselves. Their struggle was useless.

They heard Croesus call out, 'Have you got a match, Joe? I don't seem to have one.'

'I haven't got one,' said Joe angrily. 'Haven't you got a lighter or something?'

'No, nothing at all.'

'Crazy idiot,' yelled Joe in frustration. 'How can we set this house on fire without a match?'

'Don't you call me a crazy idiot, you fat fool. You are just as much to blame as I am.'

The two men started to argue furiously between themselves. Then Croesus suddenly cried out, 'Look – there's a car coming this way.'

'Not one car,' Joe shouted at him. 'There's three cars. Come on. Let's get out of here.'

Susan and Taka Taka looked at each other in relief. The taxi driver had come to their rescue. They were going to be saved after all. They heard Croesus's car start up and then they heard a crash of metal as two cars collided. A shot was fired and there was a great deal of shouting.

Then someone called out, 'They must be in the house. Be careful – there's a terrible smell of petrol.'

Moments later the sitting-room door crashed open. Four policemen burst inside and immediately started to untie Susan and Taka Taka Tom.

'Don't worry, kids. You're all right now.'

'As long as you don't light up a cigarette,' said Susan as the rag was removed from her mouth.

6
What a Hero!

Two weeks later, Ken, Tiny, Taka Taka Tom and Susan were once more sitting in the soccer stadium. They were waiting for the start of the replay of the final. The Black Eagles and the All Stars soccer teams were going to meet again!

A great deal had happened since the last match. Joe, Croesus and the doctor had all been arrested and were awaiting trial. They were bound to receive long prison sentences. When the full facts of the drugging of Shomate were revealed, the Football Association ruled that the final must be replayed. The Black Eagles and the All Stars agreed to do this.

The names of the four children had been headlined in the local newspapers. They were heroes and this time they had not had to queue to get into the ground. They had been escorted into the VIP box by the chairman of the Football Association himself! They were not sitting on wooden benches. Four armchairs had been provided for them.

The four children leaned forward in their chairs as a great roar went up from the crowd. The two teams were running on to the pitch. Shomate was leading the Black Eagles. Suddenly he stopped for a moment and waved to the children in the VIP stand. Ken, Taka Taka, Tiny and Susan stood up and waved back. They had never felt so proud in all their lives.

The chairman leaned over towards them. 'I know the full story of what you all did and I want to congratulate you,' he said. 'You are wonderful children, a fearless lot.'

Suddenly, Ken had an idea. 'We're the Fearless Four,' he said. 'That's what we're going to call ourselves from now on.'

'And Susan is the most fearless one of us all,' said Taka Taka Tom. 'If it hadn't been for Susan we wouldn't be sitting here now.'

The chairman laughed. 'The Fearless Four. I like that! It's a very good name for the four of you.'

They looked back towards the field. Not everyone seemed to have forgiven Shomate for his performance in the previous match. There was even some booing from a section of the crowd as he took up his position in the Black Eagle goal.

The whistle blew and the All Stars kicked off. Their centre-forward pushed the ball gently towards his inside-right who quickly tapped it back to the centre-half. A long shot found the left-wing who dodged around the Black Eagle right-half. Moments later the field was clear. The quick start by the All Stars had taken the Black Eagles by surprise. They were all in the wrong positions as the All Star left-wing sped towards their goal. His shot at goal was deadly accurate. Shomate dived to his left but he had no chance. The ball thudded into the back of the net. The All Stars had scored in the first minute. The crowd went wild!

Poor Shomate. He had been shamed all over again, although the shot had been impossible to save. Once again the booing

started. This time it was louder than the shouts of support.

Ken looked at Tiny in dismay. 'I hope Shomate's not going to let the team down again,' he said.

The Black Eagles quickly recovered from this set-back and launched attack after attack against the All Star goal. But they had been unsettled by the early goal and their shooting was wild. They hit the crossbar on a number of occasions. At other times they sent the ball sailing over the top of the net and into the crowd.

The All Stars fought back. Shomate made two good saves but the crowd was still not satisfied. Every time he touched the ball the booing began. Half time and the score was still one-nil to the All Stars. The Eagles were booed off the field.

When they returned for the second half, the Fearless Four stood up and yelled, 'Come on, Eagles! Come on, Shomate!'

The second half began at a furious pace. The Black Eagles had control of the ball nearly all the time but still could not find the back of the net. Their shooting was still wild and their fans were losing patience. Twenty minutes of the second half had gone by. Then a long boot down field by an All Star defender sent the ball to Shomate. There was a strange look in his eyes as he trapped the ball with his foot and then started to run with it up the field.

'Hey, Shomate! What are you doing?' his captain called out. 'Have you gone crazy, man? Don't leave your goal.'

Shomate didn't answer. Maybe he didn't hear. He swerved, side-stepped, avoided a tackle, ran round an All Star defender and in moments was in the All Star penalty area. His action had been so quick that everyone, including his own team mates, had been taken by surprise.

Then he shot at the All Star goal. It wasn't a particularly good shot, but never had the ball been hit with such power. It went straight to the All Star goalkeeper. But the strength behind the shot sent him staggering backwards with the ball in his arms. He fell over the line. It was a goal! Shomate, the Black Eagle goalkeeper, had scored by sheer force. The crowd went mad with delight. There was no more booing after that – Shomate's goal had seen to it. He had shown his own forwards how to shoot straight.

The Black Eagles now played as they had never done before. As if by magic their shooting improved. First one goal. Then two. Then three.

When the final whistle was blown they had won five-one and Shomate was the hero of the day.

His team mates carried him off the field shoulder-high. The Black Eagle supporters roared their approval. Shomate had inspired the team with his performance. He had made sure they won.

'What a match!' said Ken. 'What a fantastic match. Let's all go back to the Daystar to celebrate.'

'Can I come too?' asked Susan.

Ken looked at her and smiled. 'Of course you can,' he said, clapping her on the back. 'You can come anywhere with us. You're one of the Fearless Four.'

Tiny suddenly had an idea. He turned to the chairman of the Football Association and said, 'Would you like to come to the inter-schools' final next Saturday, sir? Our school, Westview Academy, is playing in the final. We would be honoured if you would come to watch the match.'

'Yes, of course I will,' replied the chairman. 'I would be delighted to attend. Are you in the team, Tiny?'

There was an embarrassed silence. 'Well, yes and no,' Tiny Tantille replied.

'Yes and no? What do you mean?'

'Well, I was in the team but something happened.'

'He's our star player,' Ken burst in. 'But he upset one of the masters who was refereeing the match and he's been banned from playing in the final.'

'What did you do?'

When Tiny told the chairman what had happened in the game and afterwards with Mr Juroge, he burst out laughing.

'I'm sure you said what you did in the heat of the moment,' the chairman said with a smile. 'I think that your master will let you play. Especially after what you have done to bring those criminals to justice.'

'It was Susan who did it,' said Tiny.

'I know, but Susan's part of a team. The Fearless Four. In a team, everyone gets the credit when a match is won. The credit is shared by all of you, even though Susan was the star.'

'Do you think ...' Tiny began.

'Do I think that I can persuade Mr Juroge to put you back in the team? Is that what you were going to ask me?'

'Yes.'

'I'll try but I cannot promise anything.' The chairman's eyes twinkled. 'I think you stand a good chance of getting back your place in the team. I hope to come to Westview next Saturday to watch you play. Meanwhile, I'll have a word with Mr Juroge and the headmaster on your behalf.'

'Thanks so much.'

'It's the Football Association that needs to thank all of you. We are really grateful. The least I can do is to help Tiny to take part in the final. Who else is playing?'

'I am,' replied Ken. 'I'm the goalie.'

'And your hero is Shomate, I am sure of that.'

'Yes, exactly.'

The chairman laughed. 'Just you make sure that no one tries to drug you before the match,' he said with a smile.

'Don't worry, my three team-mates will look after me,' said Ken.

They all shook hands. The Fearless Four were delighted with this conversation. On top of everything else, the chairman had lent them his chauffeur-driven car to take them to the Daystar.

7
Well Done, Fearless Four

The chairman was as good as his word. On the following Monday, Tiny was asked to report to the headmaster. Mr Juroge was in the office with him when Tiny walked in.

'I have been asked by the chairman of the Football Association to think again about something,' he began. 'The ban on you playing in the inter-schools' final next Saturday.'

Tiny Tantille said nothing as the headmaster continued, 'Having discussed the matter with Mr Juroge, we have agreed to let you play.'

Mr Juroge did not look as though he agreed with the decision at all. But he muttered, 'Yes,' under his breath.

'The school is grateful for the part you played in the arrest of dangerous criminals. However, you must not think that this excuses you from what you said to Mr Juroge last month. Have I made myself clear?'

'Yes, sir. Thank you, sir.'

'Good. Well, run along. I expect to see you make sure that Westview Academy wins the match,' he added with a smile.

'I will try my best, sir.'

'Oh, and by the way. Mr Juroge will be the match referee. You will give him the respect that he deserves.'

'Yes, sir.'

Tiny ran from the room. His friends were waiting outside for him.

'Are you going to be allowed to play?' Ken asked.

'Yes,' replied Tiny. 'I'm back in the team.'

'That's great!' Susan said. 'Let's go and celebrate.'

'Mr Juroge's going to be the referee,' Tiny said gloomily. 'We're not only playing against Hillcrest. We have to play against Mr Juroge as well.'

'Keep quiet or he'll overhear you. Then you'll be banned all over again,' said Taka Taka

Tom in alarm. He pulled Tiny down the corridor and away from the headmaster's room.

There was a good crowd on the playing field of Westview Academy when the match started on the following Saturday. News had spread that two of the four who had brought Joe, Croesus and the doctor to justice were playing. Many of the spectators had nothing to do with either Westview or the other team, Hillcrest. They had come out of curiosity. The fact that the chairman of the Football Association was there as well, had also made sure of a large crowd.

When Westview ran on to the field they were greeted with a roar of support. The Hillcrest supporters were equally noisy. Everyone thought that it would be a very close match.

The two teams lined up, Mr Juroge blew his whistle, and the schools' final was under way. Hillcrest had a strong team. For forty minutes the two teams battled against each other without success. The play swung from one end of the pitch to the other. There were not many shots at either goal. However, Ken made two wonderful saves that would have made Shomate proud of him. Tiny, who was playing on the right wing, was not given much of the ball. His only shot at goal went over the top of the crossbar. When the halftime whistle went there was no score by either side. Tiny was disappointed with the way he had been playing.

'You must pass the ball to your wingers,' the Westview captain said to his team during the interval. 'Pass the ball to Tiny. He has hardly touched it the whole match. Pass the ball and don't try to do everything on your own.'

The problem was that the mid-field players were trying to score goals on their own. They had forgotten that they were part of a team. It had been a disappointing first half.

The second half was very different. The Hillcrest team had also had a talk from their captain. Both teams suddenly came to life and play started at a furious pace. First the Hillcrest forwards attacked. Their centre-forward raced towards the Westview goal. There was no defender in the penalty area except for Ken. He hesitated a moment. Should he stay put or rush out to meet the attacker?

'Go for it,' he said to himself and rushed out towards the attacking centre-forward. The Hillcrest player paused to shoot. But he paused too long. Ken saw what he was about to do, blocked the shot, swept up the ball and booted it to Tiny on the right wing. The crowd roared in delight. What a wonderful piece of playing!

It was Tiny's turn to be inspired. He ran straight down the wing, dodged two diving tackles, ran a ring around the Hillcrest rightback and lobbed the ball neatly over the opponent's head to the Westview centre-forward. He shot. It was a goal.

The roar from the crowd blotted out a shrill blast on the whistle from Mr Juroge.

'Offside,' Mr Juroge shouted. 'Offside.'

'Whose side are you on?' muttered Tiny Tantille under his breath.

The Westview supporters groaned in disappointment. But the groans didn't last long. The free kick sailed past the Westview defenders and another dangerous attack by Hillcrest was under way. Two forwards were passing the ball back and forth and bearing down on Ken Kubwa. Ken had to make a snap decision. Should he move to the left or to the right?

'Go left,' a voice inside him said.

He did so. The long curving shot fell safely into his arms.

The chairman turned to the headmaster and said, 'That boy is good. One day he will take the place of Shomate.'

There were three minutes left to play, with still no score by either side.

Susan and Taka Taka Tom were standing together on the right-wing. 'Come on, Tiny,'

Susan called out. 'Do it for the Fearless Four.'

Tiny heard her but said nothing. If only they would give me the ball and let me have one last chance to score, he thought.

All at once the moment that he had been waiting for arrived. The Hillcrest centre-half made a bad pass to his left-wing. The winger missed the ball and it rolled towards Tiny.

'Come on, Tiny! You can do it,' the Westview supporters yelled.

Tiny scooped up the ball and ran with it as fast as he could. Once again the speed of his long legs was too much for his opponents. There was one minute of playing time left. It was now or never. He saw the open goal and the nervous Hillcrest goalkeeper hesitating as to what to do.

Don't get yourself offside, he said to himself. Be careful. Juroge is watching you.

He darted to the left to confuse the Hillcrest goalkeeper. Then he paused, aimed for the corner of the net and hit the ball with his right foot as hard as he could.

Suddenly a figure appeared from nowhere. Mr Juroge, in his anxiety to see whether Tiny was offside, had dashed across the goal mouth. The ball was going straight towards him. He was blocking the shot.

'Oh, no! Not again. Get out of the way, you idiot,' Tiny yelled.

This time Mr Juroge didn't hear him. He tripped and fell. The ball flew over his outstretched body and into the net. Westview Academy had won the match.

The Westview supporters went wild. Tiny was carried shoulder-high from the ground. Ken was also carried off on the shoulders of his team-mates.

'Well done, the Fearless Four!' shouted Taka Taka Tom and Susan.

Well done, indeed . . .

If you enjoyed reading *The Fearless Four*, you may also like to read these other stories about exciting adventures that the four friends have together.

The Fearless Four: Hijack!

John Hare

Things are getting dangerous in Gombe. There are robbers around, and they'll steal anything from a cap to a car. Tiny Tantille sets off to rescue his friend's hat and ends up fighting for his life. Thank goodness he has one of Mr Mugi's wonder pens, and three good friends. Together they are truly the Fearless Four!

Turn to the next page to read the opening few pages from this book.

1
The Wonder Pen

'Come and look! Come and look! Come and look at the pen which is mightier than the sword. It costs you nothing except your seeing power. To see is to believe. Come and look and wonder. Wonder at the power of this mighty pen.'

The salesman rolled his eyes, pulled a pen out of his pocket and twirled it round and round in his hand. He was standing on the corner of a narrow street, with a piece of metal lying on the ground in front of him. He had no idea that this township was home to a group of children known as the Fearless Four. Or that they would lead him into such danger. Perhaps he would have packed up his pens and crept away if he could have seen into the future.

The salesman was a small, slim man, dressed in a suit at least three sizes too big for him. A brown hat with a large brim was perched on the back of his head. He had a thin, hooked nose like a vulture's beak. His eyes were never still. They darted from side to side, always looking for new customers. Sometimes he would open his eyes wide and roll them around to make people stare at him.

'Look, look, look,' the salesman called out. 'Come one, come all. Come and look at the amazing pen. The pen which can pierce metal. The pen which –' He paused to take a drink from a can of Coke.

A small crowd had gathered round him.

'Get on with it,' a burly man called out. 'Stop all the talk and give us some action.'

The salesman stared at him. 'What's your hurry?' he asked. 'All in good time, my friend. No hurry in Africa.' He paused to roll his eyes. 'Patience, my friend, is the wooooooorld's medicine.'

Seeing that some people in the crowd were beginning to lose interest, the salesman decided that now was the time to act. He placed the Coke tin on the sheet of metal and grasped the ballpoint pen in his right fist like a dagger. He brought the pen crashing down on to the empty tin. It pierced it. He did this again and then again until the tin was full of jagged holes. Then he tossed the tin to one side and picked up a hammer which had been placed on the ground beside the sheet of metal. With a 'bang' he brought the hammer crashing down on top of the pen.

He looked up at the crowd and rolled his eyes once again. 'To see is to believe,' he cried out. There was another bang as the hammer fell a second time. 'One more time?' the salesman shouted. 'Yes, one more time,' the crowd roared back.

Bang, bang, bang.

'There you are, that's three more times. See how I reward your watchfulness. Now, look you all at this. I, Mr Mugi, will show you a miracle.'

The man pulled a piece of paper from his pocket and spread it out on the metal. Then he wrote the words, 'This is the wonder pen.'

'You see, no damage. A perfect pen in spite of the terrible treatment that I have banged upon it.' He stood up and showed the paper to the crowd. 'Who wants to write with the wonder pen? Who will try it out for me?'

A tall boy at the back of the crowd shouted, 'I will.' It was Tiny Tantille.

'OK, son. Come and try it.'

Tiny pushed his way to the front of the crowd and picked up the pen. 'Can I borrow the hammer?' he asked Mr Mugi.

'Sure you can, son. But don't hit your finger instead of the pen.'

The crowd laughed. Tiny grabbed the hammer and brought it down hard on top of the pen. Then he stabbed the pen on the piece of metal and the Coke tin.

He took the pen and wrote his name on the piece of paper. The pen worked perfectly.

'How much does it cost?' Tiny asked. He only had a few coins in his pocket.

'To you, son, a special, special price. A gift for the tall boy.' The salesman named a small sum, which Tiny could just afford. Then he spread out his hands and stared at the crowd. 'A gift, a gift, an absolute gift.'

Tiny handed him the money and took the pen. He pushed his way back through the crowd. As he did so, others pushed their way to the front to look at the wonder ballpoint pen.

Tiny's friend Ken Kubwa looked up at him and laughed. 'I expect it will fall to pieces in no time,' he said. 'Can I see it?'

Tiny handed him the pen as they strolled away from the crowd. Ken examined it carefully. It was unmarked. 'I wonder what it's made of?' he exclaimed. 'It's tougher than steel.'

'I don't know what it's made of,' said Tiny, 'but it's a bargain as far as I can see. You never know when it might come in useful.'

'Come on, let's get on,' said Ken. 'Susan and Tom will be wondering what has happened to us. We should have been at the Daystar half an hour ago.'

Tiny, Ken, Susan Saito and Taka Taka Tom were the four friends who had come to be known as the Fearless Four. They had earned that name after their first adventure. Then, they had uncovered a plan to fix the result of the local soccer final.

Tiny and Ken hurried through the narrow streets until they reached the Daystar, the favourite meeting place of the Fearless Four. As they entered the eating house they both gasped at the scene in front of them. Tables had been overturned and chairs were strewn about everywhere. It looked as though a fight had taken place. All at once they heard sobbing coming from one corner of the bar. It was Annie, the owner of the Daystar. Her head-tie was draped around her shoulders and her hair was ruffled and unbrushed. She was sitting on the ground, sobbing. Susan and Taka Taka Tom were kneeling beside her, trying to comfort her. Susan had an arm draped around Annie's broad shoulders.

'It will be all right, Annie,' said Susan softly. 'Don't worry, everything will be all right.'

'They have taken everything. They have taken the stock, the money – everything, just everything.' Annie began to sob again. 'I am ruined,' she cried out.

'What's happened?' asked Tiny in alarm. 'What's been going on here?'

'She's been robbed,' said Susan. 'A gang of six men attacked the bar at three o'clock this morning. They broke open the safe and took all Annie's money.'

'They had guns,' said Tom. 'There was nothing that Annie could do.'

'They tied me up,' cried Annie. 'Tied me up and threatened to kill me. This town is terrible,' she wailed. 'No one is safe any more. No one. Not even good God-fearing ladies like me. I try to earn a respectable living. This place is bad. It's rotten!'

'Have you called the police?' asked Ken.

'The telephone line was cut but someone has gone to call them. They should be here soon,' Susan replied.

Even as she spoke they heard two vehicles draw up outside the Daystar. Within minutes, three policemen had run inside. Annie looked up at them crossly.

'Innocent people like me are being robbed every night,' she cried out. 'When will you start to do something about it?'

'Cool down, lady,' said a burly sergeant. 'Don't abuse us. We're here to help you.'

'Help me! Help me! You couldn't help a sick baby,' Annie retorted.

'A lot of people need our help just now,' the policeman told her sternly. 'Haven't you heard about all the cars being stolen around here?'

'I guess we'll leave you to it, officer,' said Taka Taka Tom. 'There's no need for us to stay here any longer.'

The Fearless Four and the Graveyard Ghost

John Hare

Taka Taka Tom is delighted when he gets a holiday job but what a job! Working for an undertaker in a graveyard isn't Susan and Ken's idea of fun. Soon though, Susan, Ken and Tiny Tantille are too busy solving a mystrey to worry about Tom. Their classmate, Rich Kimani, has disappeared and they're determined to help his auntie find him. The search for Rich takes them off to the graveyard – and straight into the path of the graveyard ghost.

The Fearless Four and the Smugglers

John Hare

How can three people vanish into thin air? That is the mystery Susan Saito stumbles across on a train journey back to her home in Gombe. If her three friends are afraid to follow her into danger, then she'll just investigate on her own. Could this mean the end of the Fearless Four?